An exemplary hospital for five centuries

The Hotel-Dieu (general hospital) is the most beautiful building in the town of Beaune: following the will of its founder, Nicolas Rolin, and his wife, Guigone de Salins, it was intended to accommodate the poor, the destitute and the sick.

This exemplary hospital has federated other hospital facilities in Beaune and its surrounding areas: this explains how the hospital establishment took on the name of the Hospices of Beaune, the Hotel-Dieu being its jewel. Throughout its existence and even today, this former hospital has been benefitting from donations and bequests, which have, in particular, helped it to establish a vineyard of over 60 hectares of the best Burgundy wines.

Today, the Hospices of Beaune have maintained their hospital activities, which they perform in a modern environment a few hundred metres away from the Hotel-Dieu: as such, they constitute a prestigious institution that is very original yet hardly known in terms of its contemporary reality: the Hospices of Beaune are a health facility, and they are also the owners of a historic monument, the Hotel-Dieu, which no longer treats patients but welcomes over 400,000 visitors per year, and a prestigious vineyard which markets its production in the context of the most famous wine auction.

The substantial revenues produced by these assets provide the health facility with the means to pursue a dynamic investment policy, which are key for the renewal of its medical equipment and the comfort of its facilities.

By choosing to build a "Palace for the Poor", Nicolas Rolin allowed his charitable work to take on a perpetual character, which Beaune's patients can still benefit from today.

ANTOINE JACQUET
Director of the Hospices of Beaune

Sommaire

4 Timeline of the Hospices

8 Biography: Nicolas Rolin

10 The Hotel-Dieu's architecture

14 Roof tiles and floor tiles

16 Details and ornaments

20 Guided tour

28 The polyptych of the Last Judgement

34 The collections

40 The Hospices' wine auction

42 Useful information

COVER
General view of the Hotel-Dieu's "Courtyard of Honour".

BACK COVER
View of the Founders' Courtyard through the grid created in 1786.

LEFT PAGE
The Hotel-Dieu's courtyard with a view of the well in the foreground as well as the polychrome geometric-shaped roof decor.

SIX MAIN EPISODES FOR SIX CENTURIES OF HISTORY

Highlights of the Hotel-Dieu's history

BY CLAUDE POMMEREAU

1407: Burgundy, an ally of England

During the Hundred Years War, in the early 15th century, the dukedom of Burgundy was enriched thanks to the interplay of the Flanders and Hainaut marriages. Duke John the Fearless, a cousin of Charles VI, the king of France that went mad, had the king's brother (Louis of Orleans) murdered in 1407. From this date on, France found itself in the middle of a battle between the Armagnacs, supporters of the Orleans people and the king, and the Burgundians. In 1415, in Agincourt, the French nobility was decimated and the king of England invaded the north of France, claiming the succession of Charles VI. When England's king, Henry V, arrived in Calais, John the Fearless sided with him. Assisted by his faithful lawyer Nicolas Rolin, John the Fearless took control of Paris in 1418 but was assassinated a year later by the soldiers of the Dauphin of France during an attempted reconciliation.

1435: peace with the king of France

The new duke of Burgundy, known as Philip the Good, appointed Nicolas Rolin chancellor. The chancellor's took on the role of prime minister and was responsible for paying the Burgundian troops during this endless war against the French. Philip the Good, an ally of the English, did not hesitate to deliver Joan of Arc to them after her capture during the siege of Compiegne. Jeanne had provoked him by having Charles VII crowned in Reims. Later, in 1435, upon sensing a reversal of the situation, Philip the Good and Rolin decided to make peace with the king of France, and this in turn angered their English allies.

1441: the chancellor's fabulous project

In 1441, Nicolas Rolin and his wife Guigone de Salins decided to build a hotel-Dieu in Beaune in order to tend to the poor and the sick. To achieve this, Nicolas Rolin purchased land in the heart of Beaune for over ten years. In 1443, and before the collegiate church of Notre-Dame in Beaune, the chancellor dictated the following document to his notaries regarding the founding of the future hospital: "I,

To the left of the courtyard of Honour, the building which houses the Grand Hall of the Poor and the chapel; in the back, the well; on the right, the wing which was covered with polychrome tiles during the early 20th century restoration.

citizen of Autun [...] chancellor of Burgundy, this Sunday and fourth day of August, the year 1443 of our Lord: forsaking every affection and solicitude for worldly things, and turning my thoughts in regard to my own salvation, desire for a blissful commerce, to exchange my worldly goods which were granted to me by divine goodness [...] now and forever I am erecting and ordering the construction with endowment of a hospital in the city of Beaune for the welcoming, use and housing of poor sick people [...]."

The annual revenue which he endows the hospital with comes from income earned by the large salt works of Salins and amounts to 1000 Tours pounds. The chancellor committed to funding the building's facilities, he determined the number of beds (30), the fitting of the chapel, the assistance to the sick by "devout women of good conduct", the appointment of a master (either ecclesiastical or secular), who can be terminated at any time by himself or his heirs. In order to perfect the achievement of his "work of mercy", he ordered an altar of an amazing length (5.5 metres!) from a great artist - Rogier van der Weyden - for the chapel's high altar. For the Easter of 1446, he concluded an agreement with the carpenters of Beaune for the construction of the roof overlooking the Grand Hall of the

On the last day of the year 1451, the building constructed with a flamboyant Gothic style was finally inaugurated by its founder, chancellor Rolin.

Poor, the sisters' dormitory and the vestry (sacristy). In 1448, the hospital forms the complete U that we now see, with three buildings, the north-east one on Halles street, the south-east one along Cordeliers street and the south-west one along the city walls. The Bouzaise, which was diverted, flows beneath the courtyard and is used as a sewage system. On 31 December 1451, three and a half years later than planned, the building constructed with a flamboyant Gothic style was finally inaugurated by its founder.

1455: the early days of the Hotel-Dieu

The duke of Burgundy, amazed during his visit, granted the hospital with free use of his forests in Borne and Champ-Jarley and he authorised them to be entitled to the donations and bequests of patients who lived their final days there. Nicolas Rolin eventually negotiated the purchase of the mills next to the hospital so that they could be supplied with bread at the lowest cost possible. In 1459, having observed that Alardine Gasquierre, the nuns' teacher, imposed strict discipline upon the sick and the sisters - which is incompatible with Christian compassion - he stripped her of her responsibilities and took the opportunity to establish rules that were quite indulgent in terms of the nuns' daily lives. The Hotel-Dieu's nuns adopted his original rules as they were free from perpetual vows. A new community was born: the hospital nuns of Beaune's Hotel-Dieu, and it was officially recognised by Pius II that year. Around fifty communities were then founded in France, Switzerland and Africa. Upon his death in 1462, Guigone de Salins had to fight against his step-son, the cardinal of Autun, for six years in order for his right to the Hotel-Dieu's patronage to be recognised. She settled there and died there in 1470.

ABOVE
Peter Paul Rubens
Portrait of Charles the Bold,
duke of Burgundy
Approximately 1618, oil on canvas, 118.5 x 102 cm
Kunsthistorisches Museum collection, Vienna
© Luisa Ricciarini/Leemage
Killed in 1477, Charles the Bold was the last
Duke of Burgundy.

RIGHT
Old postcard showing an attempt to restore the
medieval roof, approximately 1890.

Hôtel Dieu - La Cour d'honneur   Beaune

1658: the visit of Louis XIV

Upon the death of Charles the Bold, the last duke of Burgundy, defeated in Nancy in 1477, king Louis XI of France regained control of Burgundy and confirmed the privileges of the Hotel-Dieu in Beaune. In 1645, thanks to a gift by a bourgeois, a new room was opened at the Hotel-Dieu, the Saint-Hugues room, decorated with murals depicting Christ's miracles. On 19 November 1658, Louis XIV visited the hospital and made a very prude request: that sick men and women no longer live together. The Saint-Hugues room was reserved for men and the Grand Hall of the Poor for women. In 1659, the lack of space forced management to undertake the building of a grain barn, rebuilt between 1736 and 1738; referred to as "the attics", it closed off the second courtyard on the south side. Thereafter, they had to create additional rooms to accommodate patients, such as the Saint Joseph room around 1830.

1971: Hotel-Dieu opens its doors to visitors

In 1971, construction of the new Philip the Good hospital, in the northern part of the city, put an end to the health care services at Hotel-Dieu. The museum extended itself to all of the 15th century buildings. In 1984, the Saint-Hugues and Saint-Nicolas rooms, where elderly patients still live, and the 15th century kitchen, were decommissioned and renovated in order to welcome visitors in 1988. Since then, considerable renovation work was undertaken, with the assistance of Historical monument funding, notably from 2007 to 2009 for the renovation of the building's beautiful slate roof which faces the street.

Joseph Bail
Preparation of Dinner
with the Hospital Ladies
1902, oil on canvas. Private collection
© Heritage images/Leemage
The nuns wear the traditional dress established by Nicolas Rolin in the rules of 1459.
This garment is derived from noble women's fashion in the mid-15th century.

20 JANUARY 1442 NICOLAS ROLIN ACQUIRES HIS FIRST PARCEL OF LAND IN BEAUNE

By creating the Hotel-Dieu, the chancellor aims to save his soul

BY CLAUDE POMMEREAU

When he was thinking about establishing the Hotel-Dieu, Nicolas Rolin was 64 years old, a very old age at the time. His success was amazing. Born in Autun, he studied both civil and canon law. A councillor of the ducal parliament of Beaune at the age of 25, he later became a lawyer in Paris, serving the duke of Burgundy, who appointed him chancellor on 5 December 1422.

Since that date, and as an all-powerful adviser, he participated in all negotiations between three irreconcilable clans: the Armagnacs, who support Charles VI (the king of France), the English, who settled north of the Loire, and the Burgundians. The Burgundy duchy's territories stretch from Holland to the gates of Switzerland and Savoy.

During the Hundred Years War, the chancellor experienced only violence, betrayal and looting. He first pushed for an alliance with the English, whose support would help him take control of Paris. This was achieved after Henry V's victory at Agincourt, which allowed John the Fearless to conquer the city. Rolin changed sides in 1435. Joan of Arc saved Charles VII's kingdom: it became time to advise his duke to make peace with the French. In this year of 1440, his wife Guigone de Salins, only 40 years old and very pious, asked him: will he be able to escape God's punishment when his time to leave the earth has come? Can he still hope for a modest share of paradise? His wealth, due to his friendship with the duke, had

become legendary. He owned many castles, parcels of land, vineyards and forests. His wife begged him to save his soul.

In these troubled times, Burgundy is travelled over by groups of armed robbers and soldiers dismissed because none of the three sovereigns' official armies can afford to pay them. Those known as the "skinners" burn, rape and rob, and the duke's loyal troops cannot stop them. The plague, the epitome of misfortune, emerged. Beggars invaded the towns of Beaune and Autun. This was the path that would lead chancellor Rolin to his salvation: why not use part of his fortune to serve the poor and the

sick? After much hesitation, he chose Beaune, a town that needed it the most. This was where he built a Hotel-Dieu. The respected lawyer made sure to first ask the pope for permission, which he received in the form of a bubble of consent in September 1441.

On Saturday, 20 January 1442, Rolin bought a first parcel of land located along the Bouzaise river, near the covered market, from Sir Guillaume of Vienna. Later on, the municipality completed this first purchase by selling him other parcels of land adjacent to his. Meanwhile, Guigone de Salins requested the Pope's exceptional authorisation to visit the religious communities in order to learn about their rules and how they operate, which Eugene IV willingly agreed to. Thanks to this initiative, a new community of women was born at the Hotel-Dieu: Beaune's hospital nuns. As would be the case with any person of his age at that time, Nicolas Rolin knew that his time was running out. He planned for the work to be completed within five years: it took three and a half years more. Nevertheless, on 31 December 1451, the chancellor, aged 75, was present for the Hotel-Dieu's inauguration.

Rogier van der Weyden
Portrait of Nicolas Rolin
Detail of the closed Last Judgement polyptych (see pg. 30)
Hotel-Dieu museum collection, Beaune © Hotel-Dieu in Beaune
The chancellor maintained close relations with the Flemish masters, as Flanders was part of the duke of Burgundy's possessions at that time.

Jan Van Eyck, The Madonna of Chancellor Rolin
15th century, oil on wood, 66 x 62 cm. Louvre collection, Paris © Photo Josse/Leemage
Nicolas Rolin commissioned this painting from Flemish painter Van Eyck during his stay in Hainaut in 1434. He owned the Aymeries castle there, which overlooked the Sambre, where the scene takes place. Some say that this was a symbol of the Burgundians' great power over the Northern States.

THE MAIN STAGES OF THE CONSTRUCTION

A palace for the poor

BY CLAUDINE HUGONNET-BERGER
Chief honorary heritage curator

On 4 August 1443, in front of Beaune's citizens, Nicolas Rolin solemnly read the founding charter of this unparalleled Hotel-Dieu which he committed to build in the heart of the city, "in proportions and with a blueprint worthy of its destination". He revealed the main points of his architectural plan: "I want it to be done in the main building, near the chapel, thirty beds, fifteen on one side and fifteen on the other, not including those that will be added to the infirmary and wherever they are needed." In order to meet the needs of patients, he planned to recruit and accommodate "devout women of good conduct".

The Hotel-Dieu's designer, whose work reflected the Flemish architectural movement, remains unknown to this day. The building, which was built within the safe walls of Beaune, on land crossed by the city's main river, the Bouzaise, is arranged around a rectangular courtyard. Combining two materials that were very expensive, freestone and slate, the building's long body - which faces the old ducal covered halls - features, to the east, the "Grand Hall of the Poor" including a chapel and, to the west, housing for the nuns featuring a dining hall, a cellar (the current ticket booth) and, upstairs, a dormitory. Dedicated to the salvation of souls and care for the body, the Grand Hall is a large hall-like room, covered with a shattered pan-

Grand Hall of the Poor: panelled barrel vault ceiling and exposed beams decorated with a backdrop painted in 1878 from the remains of medieval decor.

A detailed look at the Hotel-Dieu

1 - The arrow. It is directly above the street entrance. The community of nuns was housed to the left of the steeple (part of which is the current ticket booth). To the right, the Grand Hall of the Poor was established, followed by the chapel.

2 - The Saint Louis room. A new hall was built in 1660 for patients, right where the winepress barn was built in 1469. Now devoted to a presentation of both objects and tapestries, it also provides access to the room displaying the Last Judgment polyptych.

3 - The Hotel-Dieu's south wing. From left to right, under the glazed-tile roofs are the apothecary, the laboratory, the kitchen and the Saint-Nicolas room.

4 - The building referred to as "the attics". Completed in 1738, it was used to store grain reserves. In 1843, the Hotel-Dieu's administrators decided to call on the city's bakers. As it therefore became unnecessary, the attic building was no longer used and it was fitted with two large patient wards, the Sainte-Marguerite room and the Parizot room.

5 - The covered winepress hall. Built in the gardens in 1660, it was rebuilt in the same location in 1833 due to its age.

6 - The gallery. Built in the 15th century, it no longer exists. Initially, it gave access to two small rooms, one for the confinement of "poor frantic patients", the other one serving as a mortuary chapel.

7 - The Cemetery. No longer able to handle capacity (with a rate of 200 to 300 deaths per year in the 18th century) as it had to bury the dead "very close to each other", it was decommissioned. A new cemetery was established further south in 1756.

8 - The enclosing wall. It separated the Hotel-Dieu from the Cordeliers convent.

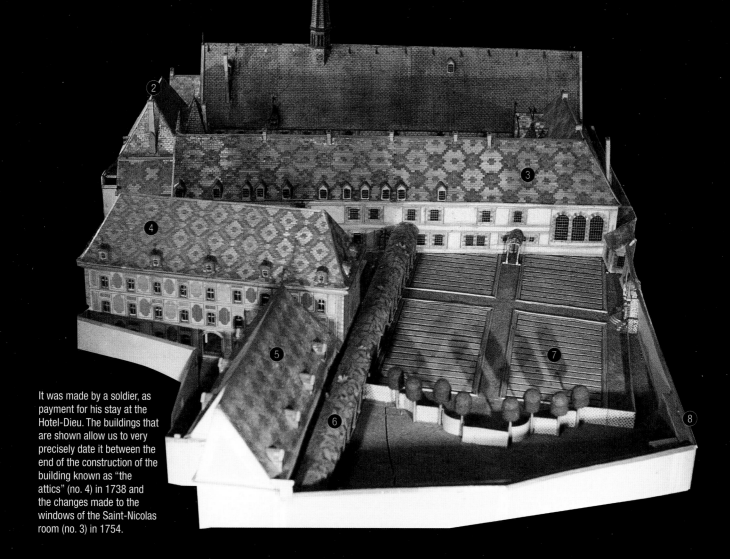

Model of the Hotel-Dieu known as the "straw hospital"

made between 1738 and 1754

It was made by a soldier, as payment for his stay at the Hotel-Dieu. The buildings that are shown allow us to very precisely date it between the end of the construction of the building known as "the attics" (no. 4) in 1738 and the changes made to the windows of the Saint-Nicolas room (no. 3) in 1754.

Octagonal spiral staircase providing access to the upper gallery, in the south-east corner of the main building.

Courtyard of Honour, where a monumental cross stood along with a pulpit built against a column of the lower gallery near the Sainte-Anne room.

The Bouzaise river played a vital role in the building's design: supplying the laundry room with water, it passed under the kitchen and the infirmary and it carried away sewage.

elled cradle that allows the framework's tie-beams and patterns to remain visible. The austerity of the main building provides a striking contrast with the colours and volumes of the L-shaped living quarters which enclose the courtyard, to the south and the east. Covered with a picturesque roof that features dormer window, the main building housed bedrooms and service rooms spread over two floors and connecting with open galleries: the infirmary for the sick in danger of death, the kitchen, the ovens, the miller, the cheese-making facility, the "salt chamber", the laundry room, the nuns' sewing room, their infirmary and eight single bedrooms. One of them was for Guigone de Salins and another one, above, was probably reserved for Nicolas Rolin. All of these rooms were covered with an exposed-beam ceiling and featured a fireplace. The winepress's barn, which was built in 1469, once existed where the Saint-Louis room now stands. Crossing through the south-west corner of the courtyard, the Bouzaise supplied water to a washhouse (demolished in 1854), before passing under the kitchen and the infirmary.

Master mason and master carpenters, building virtuosos

Although the archives remain silent regarding the name of the architect, they do reveal, however, that he is Ratheau Jehan, a master mason who oversaw the construction site. Symon Bernier, Guillemin Dudet, Guillaume La Rate and Jehannin Serreau built the trussed-rafter structure which covers the large body of the building facing the street. Baudechon Courtois, who came from the Ardennes just for this occasion, laid the slate. Jehan Digart, Jacques and Étienne Le Geot delivered the lead-glazed tiles, but it is clear that the use of tiles of various colours was not described within the archives: the multicoloured roof that contributes so much to the Hotel-Dieu's reputation were reinvented in the early 20th century by a Historical monuments architect who found inspiration in a straw model of the building, dating from the 18th century, and a renovation trial conducted around 1883.

On 1 January 1452, the Grand Hall of the Poor welcomed its first patients. Two hundred years later, the building underwent its first remodelling: in 1645, the Saint-Hugues room was fitted (in lieu of two private rooms), and then, in 1660, the winepress barn was torn down to enable the construction of the Saint-Louis room (extended to the street in 1827). In 1661, in the name of morality, it was decided that men would now be housed in the Saint-Hugues room and women in the Grand Hall of the Poor. However, the "grieving sick confinement room" remained mixed until the creation of a second infirmary, in its extension, in 1753; in its place, the Saint Nicolas room was fitted in 1847 and 1867. Rearrangements carried out in 1784 led to the disappearance of the laundry room, among other rooms, and gave way to the covered walkway next to the apothecary. In 1501, this apothecary occupied an annex of Guigone de Salins's former bedroom, and then it extended itself to the rest of this vast room which the administrators rearranged in 1776, and then fill with woodwork in 1787.

Since the early 19th century, renovation campaigns have succeeded one another. In 1872, architect Maurice Ouradou, a student and son in law of the famous Viollet-le-Duc, undertook the complete renovation of the Grand Hall of the Poor (whose chapel he had enlarged) which he fully refurnished in the Gothic revival style. The last renovation campaign, in 2007-2009, was devoted to rebuilding the slate roof, using traditional techniques.

Front door of Hotel-Dieu: double gabled canopy dominated by lead statuettes of the Virgin and Child, Saint John the Baptist and Saint Nicolas.

RIGHT PAGE
Maurice Ouradou, architect
Watercolour drawings circa 1875
1 - Cut of the Saint-Hugues room and elevation of the courtyard building covered with glazed tiles.
2 - Cross section of the chapel and elevation of the courtyard building covered with glazed tiles.

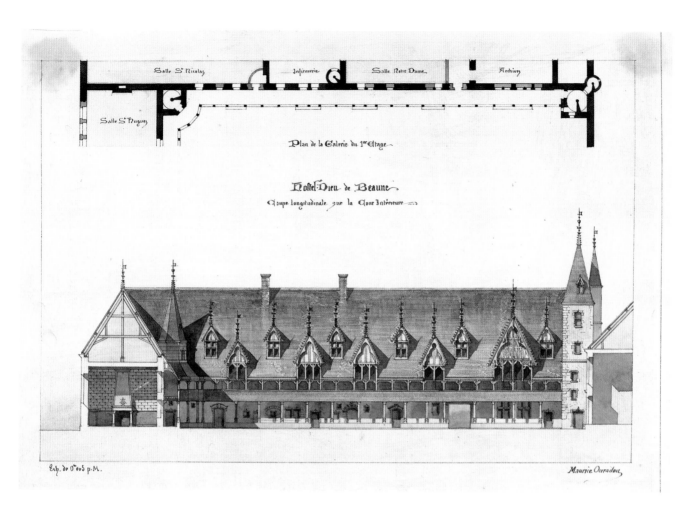

Plan de la Galerie du 1er Étage.

Hostel-Dieu de Beaune
Coupe longitudinale sur la Cour Intérieure

Salle S. Nicolas Infirmerie Salle Notre Dame Archives

Salle S. Hugues

Éch. de 0m005 p.M.

Maurice Ouradou

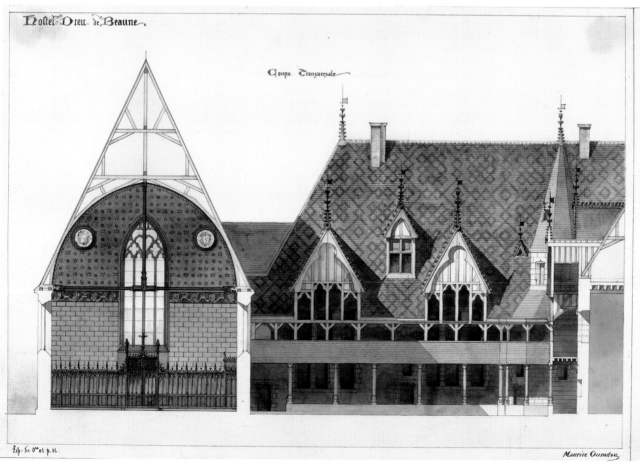

Hostel-Dieu de Beaune.

Coupe Transversale

Éch. de 0m01 p.M.

Maurice Ouradou

13

15TH CENTURY MANUFACTURING TECHNIQUES

Rediscovering ancestral knowledge

BY CATHERINE BARADEL-VALLET
Doctor of Art History

In its current state, the Hotel-Dieu is the culmination of a series of transformations spread over six centuries. However, with the exception of the large patient ward, covered with very conspicuous slate, successive buildings were all originally covered with polychrome patterns that evolved according to architectural modes. Archived records attest to the presence of "sealed tiles" from Aubigny-en-Plaine on the medieval buildings. With this in mind, Beaunoise constructions followed the example set by the Hotel-Dieu of Tonnerre, built in 1293-1295, or Paris's Saint-Jacques-aux-Pèlerins hospital, built in 1319. As is the case today, it seems that the roof tiles featured four colours (brown-red, green, yellow, black), but according to the straw model produced between 1738 and 1754, the ornamental structure rested upon a simple fishnet stamped at each intersection with a small diamond shape. The straw model also provides a reminder of the patterns placed on the Saint Louis pavilion - built in 1668 and restored in 1989 - and the Saint-Côme pavilion - dating back to 1736. Both creations had caissons arranged in staggered rows and vertically separated by small diamond shapes, which was used on a large scale in the 17th century and to a smaller extent in the 18th century. After a first attempt to restore the medieval roofs made by Felix Goin around 1890, Louis Sauvageot decided to replace the old pattern with a relatively complex composition created in 1873 by Maurice Ouradou using 17th century creations from Dijon. This characterises Beaune's Hotel-Dieu since 1907.

Renovation work of 1902-1907

The production of glazed tiles and floor tiles became so rarefied from the 18th century on that much of the technical knowledge developed during the Middle Ages has been lost. 19th century architects, committed to large renovation projects, experienced great difficulty in obtaining tiles that were resistant to visitors' steps and weather conditions. Furthermore, the mechanisation of production and the addition of tin in the glazing led to tiles with loud and bold colours. Research conducted by Louis Sauvageot during renovation work has been exemplary. He tested several companies before choosing a tile maker that had proven itself, that of Montchanin in Saône-et-Loire. Driven by the desire to restore the roofs close to their original state, he refused the standardisation offered by industrial products and demanded that the new tiles feature various shades calibrated to the chromatic scale of the former tiles. The architect was no less demanding in terms of shapes, as he wanted the new tiles to be facsimiles of the old ones, going as far as duplicating certain imperfections that resulted from manual production. The obtained visual effect was particularly balanced and harmonious.

The polychrome tiles that cover a portion of the roofs, in an arrangement defined during the 1902-1907 renovation, became a symbol of Beaune's Hotel-Dieu.

Glazed tiles exposed in the Saint-Nicolas room.

Medieval artisan production in three stages

Roof tiles and floor tiles were produced in the same workshops, using relatively similar techniques.

1 The clay extracted from the ground was stripped of its impurities through tilling and soaking before being trampled on by a worker to obtain a homogeneous material. It is possible that sand was added as a degreaser in order to reduce the risk of shrinkage during drying and baking.

2 The next stage was the moulding. For the roof tiles, this was done in a movable frame made of wood or iron, and the upper surface was then smoothed out.
One or two holes, which allowed one to attach each tile to the frame's lattice, could be made using a nail, and the suspension hook was attached to the smooth surface of the tile.
Typical roof elements usually turned their rough side toward the exterior, which is not compatible with the application of glazing.
Tiles that were intended for glazing were therefore smoothed out on both sides. In addition, there was a feature clearly visible on the roofs of the Hotel-Dieu in Beaune: the lower edges

of the tiles were cut diagonally to minimise shadows, thereby improving the aesthetic qualities of the final composition. The tiles were then left to dry, often on the ground outdoors, but always sheltered from the sun and the rain. The floor tiles were also manufactured using moulds, usually square ones. After drying for 24 hours, the decoration phase began: the tiles were then cut with a knife according to a shape's pattern or embossment. Then they were placed in direct sunlight and rain for a second drying session.

3 The final step was the application of the glazes, which consisted of mixtures of lead, sand, clay and mortar-grounded metal oxides, which vitrified during the baking process. Applied directly to the raw clay, this glass film conferred a much appreciated red-brown hue and brightness to the tiles. Depending on the dosages and cooking conditions, the addition of iron generated a range of yellows while copper generated a palette

Original terracotta tile featuring Nicolas Rolin and Guigone de Salins's initials.

of greens. However, pale yellows and light greens required the interposition of a slip (a thin layer of white or coloured clay) between the body of the tile and the glaze. The medieval artisans therefore had access to four basic colours: yellow, brown-red, green and a very dark green that was close to black. Due to the set of slips partially covering the room and the juxtaposition of differently coloured glazes, many floor tiles and some roof tiles featured two-colour patterns.

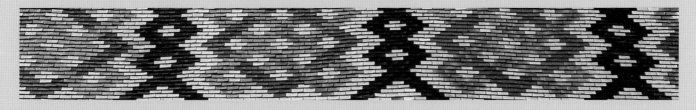

FACADES AND ROOFS

Between efficiency and ostentation

BY CLAUDINE HUGONNET-BERGER
Chief honorary heritage curator

1- *Awning sculptures in double saddle*
This elegant construction covered with slate and crowned with lead ornaments sheltered the poor who came to the door while protecting the tympanum which was then carved with a Holy Trinity. Each corner of the awning is decorated with a hanging key carved mainly with two angels with Guigone de Salins's coat of arms. The same motif adorns the centre of the roofing panels.

2- *Large dormer window, in the axis of the king's bedroom*
It helped improve the natural lighting of the room, which was darkened by the gallery. The Notre-Dame bedroom and the Dieu-bedroom enjoyed an identical configuration. Smaller dormer windows which fulfilled the same function faced the upper floor's other rooms: the infirmary and the nuns' sewing room, the cheese room and the Sainte-Catherine bedroom.

3- *Knocker*
Its enigmatic decor represents a sort of orvet eagerly watching a fly. It was rebuilt identically when architect Maurice Ouradou restored the Grand Hall of the Poor in 1872-1878. Next to the knocker, a door viewer allowed the women of the hospital to examine, without being seen, the poor who knocked at the Hotel-Dieu's door.

4- *Lead ornaments*
Painted, gilded or tin plated, these elements, which abundantly decorated the roof, also had a useful role since some of them prevented water from leaking in. The wind vanes were painted with the colours of the founder's coat of arms: "Azure with three gold keys arranged on the ends". The disappearance of most of these ornaments over time required that they be replaced in 1843.

5- *"Flemish" dormer window*
above the nuns' dormitory
The procurement contract signed in 1446 for the frame of the large street-side building mentions these "Flemish or Beauvoisines dormer windows" of which we see other examples on the L-shaped main building.

GLASS WINDOWS, FLOORS AND FIREPLACES

Between spirituality and comfort

BY CLAUDINE HUGONNET-BERGER

Chief honorary heritage curator

1- *The chapel's large glass window*

Work by the Parisian glass master Léon-Auguste Ottin (1877)
Borrowing from the iconography of the former glass window, it represents the Calvary and, on the lower part, the Virgin of mercy between Nicolas Rolin and his wife. Around the sides of the cross, we see the Virgin Mary, Saint John the evangelist, Sainte Marthe (in charge of the hospital nurses), Sainte Madeleine and Philip the Good with his wife and their son, the future Charles the Bold.

2- *Grand Hall of the Poor*

Over one hundred oak barrels, each one 14 to 16 metres long, were used to create this structure which features figurative hammer beams and girders (with ends carved into monster heads). They came from the ducal forests, especially that of Argilly. Dendrochronology has demonstrated that the trees were cut down during the fall and winter of 1446-1447, and that the structure was erected in July-August 1448. The shattered panelled cradle peaks at 15.86 metres.

3- *Floor tiles produced in 1448*

They follow a model that sculptor Jehannin Fouquerel had created for Nicolas Rolin's Dijon hotel: their decor included the NG monogram and the gallant motto "lone star", adopted by the chancellor in honour of his wife. The pavement of the Grand Hall of the Poor, which was completely redone in 1878, is partially made up of sandstone blocks that replicate the decor of medieval tiles: they were made by the Boch et Frères (Boch and Brothers) company.

4- *Hagioscope of the Dieu-bedroom*

It was thus described in 1501: "en ladicte chambre ung oratoire regardant sur le grant aultel de ladicte chapelle pour les malades à ouyr messe" ("in the said bedroom, an oratory opening up onto the said chapel's great altar for the sick of our church service"). In accordance with Nicolas Rolin's desire, two priests, housed at the Hotel-Dieu, performed a church service every morning at 8:00.

5- *Fireplace in Sainte-Anne's bedroom*

This was the only private bedroom which retained its 15th century fireplace despite all of the alterations which it was subjected to. In 1693, François Brunet of Montforand had three beds installed there provided that the patients treated here say an "Ave" and a "Pater" for the peace of his soul. Upon his death, his heart was placed in this bedroom which took on the name of the Saint Francis room. Decommissioned in 1788, it welcomed the novitiate until 1930.

1

4

ROOM AFTER ROOM, A TRIP BACK TO THE HEYDAY OF THE MIDDLE AGES

A guided tour of the Hotel-Dieu

BY RAFAEL PIC
Journalist

The opportunity to experience the interior of the Hospices is a recent privilege. The sick and the elderly occupied it until the early 1980s and the first visits, following their departure, were guided tours initially. Since 1988, however, the approximately 400,000 annual visitors can wander freely throughout the rooms. Visitors can even view Rogier van der Weyden's masterpiece, which was long reserved for the sole admiration of the patients - and only on holidays! Nevertheless, the Hotel-Dieu's beauty could be experienced through other means, some of them unexpected: for example, the scene in Don't Look Now... We're Being Shot At!, shot in 1966, which shows the British airmen who are cared for by the nuns, was seen by millions of viewers - providing the Grand Hall of the Poor an almost global audience...

The courtyard had a washhouse and several wells, including this one which was used by the kitchen.

THE GRAND HALL OF THE POOR

A revolutionary approach in terms of patient privacy

Under the vaulted oak-panelled roof which looks the hull of an upside-down boat and rises 16 metres high, it is the Hotel-Dieu's most impressive space. This room measures about 50 metres long and 14 metres wide. It could have accommodated a large number of patients but chancellor Rolin's instructions voluntarily limited the number of beds to thirty (fifteen on each side), each one accommodating two patients. Curtains ensured that the patients had privacy, especially during examinations carried out by the practitioner. Each patient had a chair, a nightstand and "luxurious" dishes as they were made out of tin instead of wood, as was the case in comparable institutions at the time. And although the room was not heated, hot water bottles were available to spend a warmer night... A Christ of mercy placed above the front door offered his protection, and the nuns could themselves take a look at their patients at any time through a window upstairs, where they were housed. The first patient was welcomed on 1 January 1452, however, the month was marked by a less happy event: the first death. Although infected patients were not admitted, they sometimes forced their way through the door. As a result, in 1553 and in 1628, in the middle of a plague epidemic, the municipal authorities imposed their hospitalisation, resulting in the deaths of several nuns. Renovated by architect Maurice Ouradou in 1872, the Grand Hall accommodated patients up to 1955, representing rare continuity - more than five centuries of medical care!

The stone walls and the beautiful oak beams date back to the middle of the 15th century. The beds and the chapel's closure were renovated by architect Maurice Ouradou in the second half of the 19th century.

THE CHAPEL
Here lies Guigone, the chancellor's widow

The chapel, which was consecrated on 31 December 1451 (on the eve of the arrival of the first patients), and separated from the Grand Hall of the Poor by a wooden fence reproduced by Maurice Ouradou, featured the masterpiece that Chancellor Rolin commissioned from Rogier van der Weyden. Hidden during the Revolution, the polyptych was definitively moved during its renovation by the Louvre workshops in 1875-1878, but it returned to its original location exceptionally on the occasion of the visit by president Pompidou on 29 October 1970. Although the glass structure is also a creation by

Maurice Ouradou, the high marble alter is slightly older (sculpted by Etienne de Saptes in 1845, for the four hundredth anniversary of the founding of the Hotel-Dieu). Guigone de Salins, chancellor Rolin's widow, who was buried at his feet, suffered from the revolutionary iconoclasm: as with the religious paintings or symbols of royalty, her bones were mishandled and then buried again in the chapel.

The restored windows carry the keys and the tower, the respective coat of arms of the Rolin and Salins families.

THE SAINT-HUGUES ROOM
A symbol of the generosity of donors

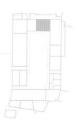

This room was converted from the Saint John the Baptist and the Notre-Dame bedrooms, which were superimposed, and refitted. As the hospices depended on the generosity of individuals, donations from rich people marked their history. This was the case with this room, which had a capacity of twelve beds and was funded in 1645 by Hugues Bétauld (a resident of Beaune), hence the name of the room. After the 1658 visit of Louis XIV, who did not like seeing such promiscuity between the sexes, the room was reserved for male patients, who would benefit from the rooms' inspirational scenes: the miracles of Christ on the walls and, on the ceiling, a large mounted canvas by Isaac Moillon featured details of the healing of the cripple at the Pool of Bethesda.

In this room, which has hardly changed since the 17th century, the decorative cycle owed to Isaac Moillon includes nine miracles of Christ, placed in frames in trompe-l'oeil fashion. The painting above the altar is devoted to the Miracle of Saint Hugues.

The episode of the healing of the paralytic in the Pool of Bethesda, appearing on the ceiling, is drawn from the Gospel of Saint John.

THE SAINT-NICOLAS ROOM

Under your feet flows the Bouzaise...

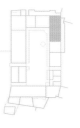

THE KITCHEN

White bread and mea

The Saint Nicolas room was originally "the Infirmary of the Poor patients who are in danger of death". We can now admire the windows depicting the construction of the buildings, the hospital nuns and the medical utensils used in the past.

Louis XIV's visit in 1658 had another consequence, much later (in 1756): the establishment of two separate infirmaries, one for men, the other for women. This room is the result of their fusion, and it was fitted during the Second Empire. Here, you can admire the straw model, made by a patient around 1740-1750, which was especially useful in helping early 20th century renovators design the polychrome roof tile patterns. Decommissioned as late as 1984 (it welcomed elderly patients until then), various instruments that summarise the medical practices of the past are on display there. At its centre, under a slab of glass, we can see the Bouzaise river flow. The Hotel-Dieu was built on it and it served as the sewage system.

The kitchen was one of the Hospices' most active areas: in any season, you had to be able to provide the sick with food, not to mention ensure the daily distribution of white bread at the door of the Hotel-Dieu, as was pointed out in a 1443 instruction. Between patients and nurses, this amounted to over a hundred people. Although the sink and stove are both recent installations, the double fireplace is the original one and the malicious rotisserie automaton, Sir Bertrand, is himself very old, having been installed in 1698 by local clockmaker Defresne. The kitchen,

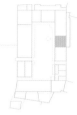

on the roaster for all!

which was subjected to various fatal events during its first century - the ceiling collapse in 1459, a fire in 1499 - was gradually reduced in size, notably due to the creation of the women's infirmary which encroached upon both of the constantly running ovens, while the flour storage room that was located upstairs was moved to another building.

With the exception of the double fireplace, the chimney hook (visible in the right hearth) and the triple rotisserie mechanism led by Sir Bertrand, the kitchen's current design is based on 17th, 18th and 19th century utensils.

THE LABORATORY

Medication, medicated plaster and other potions

At the time, medication, medicated plaster and other potions were prepared on the spot. This room was reconstituted under the invocation of Claude Morelot, an apothecary at the Hotel-Dieu, painted in 1751 by Coquelet-Souville. The artist depicts him in full action in his work area, next to his assistants who are cooking and grinding (foreground) and distilling (background) the beneficial substances. Many ingredients came directly from the institution's medicinal garden, which can be spotted in the painting's background. Some of the instruments that were used at the time are exposed, including the colossal pestle mortar (which weighs 6 kg), articulated by means of an arc, and stills. In the 18th century, the sale of inpatients' clothes was used to pay the apothecary, an external employee; however, as this income proved to be insufficient, from 1788 on this discipline once again came to be practiced by one of the nuns...

The dispensary contained a variety of materials. Here we see stills and, on the table, a suppository set, as well as a scale and cocoa butter...

Michel Charles Coquelet-Souville
Claude Morelot in his dispensary
1751, oil on canvas, 160 x 139.2 cm.
Hotel-Dieu museum collection, © Beaune
Archives Charmet/The Bridgeman Art Library

THE DISPENSARY

The secrets of the ointments

Treacle, castor powder and crayfish eyes: a wide range of sovereign remedies stored on the shelves.

In the 15th century, this was the "room-Madame", or, in other words, the room where Guigone de Salins, chancellor Rolin's widow, resided. The woodwork, which imitated the marble crafted by Joseph Bonhomme, a master carpenter in Beaune, subsequently provided it with a very different appearance. The collection of earthenware pots was probably purchased in 1789 from the last external apothecary, Claude-Étienne Grémaud. Their shapes determined their contents - syrups, waters, pills or ointments - while the glass jars, which numbered two hundred according to the revolutionary inventory of 1791, retained substances which may appear surreal to us (marshmallow powder, ambergris, divine stone, wormwood salt), but whose healing powers were held in high regard at the time.

One of the stunning 18th century earthenware pots.

THE SAINT LOUIS ROOM
The tapestry sanctuary

Created and furnished in 1660 thanks to a gift from Louis Bétauld (brother of Hugues, mentioned on pg. 23), this room housed up to twenty-six beds and was once reserved for patients with military origins. Although the friezes that decorate it feature a modern style (early 20th century), its main attraction comes from the works that are exposed there: notably the series of tapestries and hangings (History of Jacob, Parable of the Prodigal Son), which are some of the institution's treasures, as well as paintings and object collections that were donated

recently, like a wine tasting set. The Saint-Louis room also provides access to the room that is now devoted to Rogier van der Weyden's Last Judgment polyptych, which has been on display there since 1974.

This large room, which was original used for the winepress and the vats, and later for the sick in 1660, now serves as a home to everyday objects and a fine collection of tapestries.

Like the large windows, the furniture was also marked with the arms of the Hotel-Dieu's founding couple, Nicolas Rolin and Guigone de Salins.

Rogier van der Weyden, polyptych of the *Last Judgement*

An altarpiece of exceptional dimensions

BY THOMAS SCHLESSER
Art historian

The polyptych created at the request of Chancellor Rolin for the Hotel-Dieu in Beaune is one of the most distinguished masterpieces ever created by Rogier van der Weyden, founder of the great 15th-century Flemish tradition along with Jan van Eyck and Robert Campin. A Tournai native, born Roger de la Pasture, he opted for the name of Rogier van der Weyden when he became Brussels's official painter in 1435. He actively worked for the Burgundian court, where he was considered Europe's best artist after the death of van Eyck. He also made a trip to Italy.

The polyptych of the Last Judgment is a monumental piece consisting of nine oak panels, six of which are painted on both sides, 2.25 metres high and 5.50 metres wide. As there are no records, its date of completion is difficult to estimate... The altarpiece was probably present when the chapel was consecrated on 31 December 1451, but work on it evidently started after the building was founded in 1443. Thanks to archives from 1501, we know that it was placed on the Grand Hall of the Poor's chapel high altar. Van der Weyden's work had to be visible by the bedridden patients. The altarpiece was usually closed. On Sundays and holidays, the panels were unfolded, allowing a flood of striking lights and colours to escape. The composition produced a dramatic effect through its distribution of figures over three levels: the frieze of humans at the bottom, the circle of apostles and saints in the middle, whose eyes converge toward the centre, upon a pyramidal summit dominated by Jesus. The different scales reflect the undeniable influence of Van Eyck's The Mystic Lamb, painted in the 1430s. Questions of death, the afterlife and divine judgment are necessarily strong, even urgent, in a medieval hospital. In addition, it wasn't just a liturgical object intended to celebrate church services, but, anthropologically speaking, it was a therapeutic accessory that was to give back hope to the sick. The Last Judgment sought to encourage spiritual elevation through which it would become possible, according to the beliefs of the time, to improve the health of the faithful, or at least to promote their state of grace so that they could leave the physical world in peace.

A spectacular restoration

The polyptych, an impressive iconographic device, still holds some mysteries, some grey areas in terms of the possible identifications and interpretations that exist. But, above all, it is a major work of the 15th century, classified as a Historical monument since 1891. The restoration modalities which this altarpiece was subjected to are spectacular, to say the least. Hidden in an attic to escape the revolutionary destruction, it was recovered in 1836. Prudish additions to it were then discovered: the nakedness of the humans populating the bottom of the polyptych was concealed with homespun robes for the officials and flames for the damned. In 1875, the Hospices' administrators entrusted its restoration to the Louvre workshops, which proposed to cut through the thickness of the panels painted on both sides. An intervention that allows the altarpiece to be displayed in its dual configuration, open and closed.

Rogier van der Weyden
The Last Judgement
open polyptych,
detail of the central panel,
1446-1452, oil on wood,
220 x 548 cm.
Hotel-Dieu museum collection,
Beaune © Hotel-Dieu in Beaune

The closed polyptych

1- Gabriel, the announcer

The four central recesses of the closed altarpiece were processed in grisaille, like trompe-l'oeil sculptures, which immediately distinguishes sacred history from profane history (embodied by Nicolas Rolin and Guigone de Salins on the side panels). Gabriel the angel is represented here as in the Annunciation episode recounted in the Gospel according to Luke.

3- A saint against disease

Christianity is based on the traditional - and somewhat legendary - persecution of martyrs, especially those early believers who defied the Roman world before Constantine's conversion. The list of these "heroes" is long. But Saint Sebastian, pierced with arrows here when he was put to death, is one of the most popular ones of 15th century iconography because he protected people from plague epidemics.

2- The great founder

Nicolas Rolin, the founder of Hotel-Dieu, is depicted with startling realism, in a posture of prayer. An Autun native, his social ascension was fantastic, thanks to the trust of the two dukes of Burgundy from the House of Valois: John the Fearless and Philip the Good. A chancellor in 1422, he established himself as a prominent patron, a builder of castles and city residences and the founder of the Hotel-Dieu in 1443 in Beaune, his mother's hometown. Behind him, an angel bears his coat of arms: the three golden keys, two main ones and a pointed one.

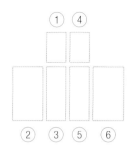

4- Mary full of grace

Mary, who is holding the Gospel, receives a message from Gabriel the angel. Beside him, a dove symbolises the Holy Spirit, who, according to Luke, unexpectedly arrives in order to allow the young virgin to give birth to Jesus, the son of God. This miraculous fertility also fulfilled the role of bringing hope to the sick of Beaune's hospital.

5- A hermit and his pig

Like Sebastian, Saint Anthony, born in the mid-3rd century, is invoked against the plague. The founder of Christian eremitism, he is especially known for his resistance to numerous diabolical temptations, such as the violent hallucinations that often inspired artists. At his feet, the saint kept his faithful companion, a pig, whose head can be seen. In the Middle Ages, the Antonin order's hospital staff had the right to let these animals wander in the streets, provided that they wore a bell. Anthony is the Hotel-Dieu's patron saint and Guigone de Salins had enormous admiration for him.

6- Guigone de Salins: an unwavering devotion

In 1423, Nicolas Rolin married Guigone de Salins, a woman of Franche-Comté nobility. Very pious and committed to helping the sick, she played an important role in the initiation of her husband's charity work. Once widowed, she ran the Hotel-Dieu until her death, after a court trial against her step-son, cardinal Jean Rolin. Behind her, and just like the panel devoted to Nicolas Rolin, her husband's coat of arms is featured on a shield carried by an angel. The Salins' crenelated tower is a reference to her ancestors.

The open polyptych

1- The weighing of souls

The central theme of the work is the weighing of souls, which is the critical moment at the end of time where all men are separated into good ones and bad ones. The figure of the resuscitated Jesus Christ, in all his glory, appears over a rainbow (a symbol of the New Alliance between God and man), presiding over the Last Judgment's grand tribunal. At his feet, under a globe symbolising the universe, Michael, the Judgment's archangel, is at work, placing individuals in the balance to separate the damned souls from those that will be saved. His expression, like that of Jesus, is frontal and unaffected.

2- A reminder of the Passion

On both panels, angels bear the instruments of the Passion, a reminder of all the terrestrial suffering that Christ had to endure for the remission of sins: we see the cross, the crown of thorns, the reed, the sponge at the end of a stick, the Roman centurion's spear and the column.

3- Mary full of grace

The Virgin and John the Baptist both form a duo of intercessors. Her face is gentle, caring, focused and concentrated on her son. And along with Jesus and John the Baptist, they form a triangle which is inversely mirrored by that of archangel Michael and the two angels bearing the instruments of the Passion.

4- John the Baptist the precursor and André the protector

John the Baptist stands at the foot of the rainbow to the left of Jesus. Historically speaking, Christian tradition has viewed this key figure, who we know was a highly influential preacher in Galilee and Judea, as a herald of Christ, the prophet who steps aside to make room for the Saviour. Behind him, we notably see Saint Andrew (in red), the first of the apostles and the protector of Burgundy, who looks at the spectacle of the damned with sadness.

5- Peter pillar of the Church

Wearing bright red that echoes the colour of the Passion, Peter was designated by Jesus as the pillar of Christianity. Beside him, John, very young and wearing white, was the Lord's favourite disciple. Behind them sat a pope, a bishop and a king. The individuals that surround Jesus have no attributes, which makes it hard to identify them, but the frankness of the colours they are wearing allowed the faithful to spot them from afar.

6- Paul, the messenger

Seated and wearing green, Paul has special status in sacred history. Once a persecutor of Christians, he experienced a revelation and a conversion on the road leading him to Damascus. Following this event, he became an extremely active messenger. Green is the colour of birth, of spring and of germination. The identity of the three saints who sit behind him remains a mystery.

7- Joy in the new Jerusalem

The dead emerging from the earth responded to the angels' trumpet calls. The chosen ones will ascend to Heaven, where they will be called to live with God. They are preparing to climb the steps of heavenly Jerusalem, whose usher is an angel. This new and beautiful city, "prepared like a bride adorned for her husband", according to John (Apocalypse 21:2), looks like a golden palace with soaring architecture.

8- Horror in the depths of Hell

The expressions on the faces of the damned are particularly harrowing. These wretched sinners that were sent to Hell have bulging eyes, their faces stretched with anguish and suffering because the fires are already burning them. Crowded together, they hold onto each other, but their fall is inevitable. The abyss, which is lined with steep and dark cliffs, contrasts with the architecture of the heavenly panel on the far left.

HANGINGS AND TAPESTRIES

Saints and heroes woven with silver thread, silk and wool

BY CLAUDINE HUGONNET-BERGER

Chief honorary heritage curator

In addition to a rare embroidered antependium, the Hotel-Dieu has retained the tapestries that Nicolas Rolin and his wife Guigone de Salins adorned it with. All of these pieces share a red or dark blue background, decorated with their coat of arms or furniture of their arms, namely Rolin's keys and Salins' towers: this set of tapestries consists of trim designed for the chapel's furniture and ceremonial blankets placed on the thirty beds of the Grand Hall of the Poor (on holidays only). Over time, the hospital acquired nearly one hundred tapestries dating back to the 16th, 17th and 18th centuries, woven in Tournai, Paris, Oudenaarde, Brussels and Aubusson for the most part.

ABOVE

Tapestry with a thousand flowers, Saint Éloi

Early 16th century

This is an assembly of elements from various works which probably belonged to the same tapestry. The central scene partially shows one of Saint Éloi's miracles, a farrier, but the saint is absent: we only see the horse and his rider. The very dense flower decor which animates the tapestry's background is filled with birds and rabbits.

LEFT

Tapestry of the Mystic Lamb

3rd quarter of the 15th century

The Hotel-Dieu has preserved two similar tapestries, both with a blue background, one serving as altar cladding, while the other larger one is used to cover the pulpit. The lamb, whose blood is flowing into a chalice, symbolises Christ's sacrifice. Behind it, we see the cross along with the other instruments of the Passion, between the sun and the moon.

ABOVE

Tapestry of Saint Anthony

3rd quarter of the 15th century
Nicolas Rolin had placed the Hotel-Dieu under the protection of this saint which he especially revered, but, in 1452, in order to avoid controversy with the Order of Saint-Anthony-en-Viennois, the pope replaced him with Saint John the Baptist. Along with Saint Sébastian and Saint Roch, Saint Anthony was one of the major "antiplague" saints, but he was specifically invoked against ergotism, known as burning sickness ergotism or Saint Anthony's fire.

LEFT

Tapestry of The Parable of the Prodigal Son

Tapestry of duck hunting, woven in 1520 in Tournai or in a workshop inspired by Tournai creations
One of the seven parts that make up this tapestry depicts a duck hunt featuring the Prodigal son on horseback, accompanied by a woman sitting behind him.

RELIGIOUS AND SECULAR OBJECTS

For the salvation of souls and the healing of body

BY CLAUDINE HUGONNET-BERGER
Chief honorary heritage curator

From the long list of art objects inventoried in 1501, only a small number of sculptures remain. However, the Hotel-Dieu retains a collection that is unique in France, thirty-five medieval chests that were used for the storage of food or linen, clothing and more valuable possessions. By the late 15th century, the Hotel-Dieu endowed itself with a dispensary, which was gradually expanded, refurbished in 1776, and then furnished with woodwork in 1787 in order to accommodate the sets of green decorated pots that are still visible there. Evidence of everyday life, the tin health care objects bear the hallmarks of Beaune or Dijon craftsmen.

Clothes chest
3rd quarter of the 15th century, oak
This austere clothing chest, of which at least three other copies existed, features Guigone de Salins's coat of arms (consisting of the Rolins's key and the Salins's tower).

Pharmacy jars, 1782, earthenware

The Hotel-Dieu has an extensive and highly original collection that was inspired by antique vases. It consists of 128 pharmacy jars, made of high-fired earthenware and featuring green decorations and snakes. Depending on their shapes, they could contain solids, such as ointments, powders and pills, or liquids such as oils and syrups.

Feeding bottle for the sick

Work by Beaune silversmith Philibert Viénot, silver, with "HOTELLE+DIEU+1668" inscribed on it

These sorts of objects, which were common in hospitals, were usually made of tin or ceramic. This one, which was exceptionally made of silver, was probably reserved for patients in private rooms. An allegory of charity adorns its lid.

Pharmacy mortar and pestle

17th-century bronze

These types of relief-decorated table mortars were commonly used in hospitals. The Hotel-Dieu has several of them, one of which was given to it in 1673 and which is decorated with medallions that feature Christ's monogram, IHS.

"Self-administered" enema syringe

19th century, tin

This type of syringe, which was very common, allowed patients to self-administer enemas. This syringe features the hallmark of Beaune pewterer Thomas Caramello.

LEFT

Saint Roch

Late 16th century, painted wood, folk art

This saint was the subject of special devotion in the countryside as he was believed to be able to prevent all epidemics, including those that threatened livestock. A victim of the plague, Saint Roch points to a bubo on his right thigh. The dog that brought him bread each day is sitting at his feet.

OPPOSITE

Christ of Pity

4th quarter of the 15th century, painted oak, probably ordered from a Flemish workshop, perhaps in Antwerp or Brussels

This statue, which has always overlooked the entrance to the Grand Hall of the Poor, is the only 15th century work that is still in place. In those days, the theme of Christ in chains, sitting on a rock and crowned with thorns, enjoyed some popularity in Europe.

DRAWINGS BY ARCHITECT MAURICE OURADOU

Pen and wash drawings for an exemplary restoration

BY RAFAEL PIC
Journalist

Maurice Ouradou
Painting of the tympanum, above the entrance doors
1882, watercolour drawing
This composition, which was supposed to replace the Trinity destroyed during the Revolution, was never made. In its place, we simply find the Hotel-Dieu's name on a black slab of marble.

Mishandled by the Revolution, the Hotel-Dieu was classified as a Historic monument in 1862. The first restoration campaigns began two decades before, on the occasion of its 400th anniversary. These campaigns intensified at the turn of the 20th century, when architect Louis Sauvageot restored the polychromatic appearance of the roofs (1902-1907). The most significant intervention of this ambitious project is attributed to Maurice Ouradou (1822-1884). This architect worked with Viollet-le-Duc, of which he was the son-in-law, at the Notre-Dame in Paris and at the collegiate Notre-Dame church in Beaune, and then succeeded him at the Pierrefonds castle. In Beaune, Ouradou drew inspiration from the highly detailed inventory of objects and furniture compiled in 1501 (still preserved in the institution's archives) when he performed a general rehabilitation of the Grand Hall of the Poor. He found himself in charge of the renovation of the paintings on the panelled ceiling, the reopening of the

chapel's axial window and the painting of decorations on the walls. To achieve all of this, Ouradou conducted an extensive study, confirmed by his numerous drawings. He admired his ability "to have been able to find, beneath the layers of successive washes, most of the main elements that made up the general decoration". He asked his craftsmen to become familiar with "the decorative style of the Middle Ages" and then entrusted Beaune's Pasquinelly-Brulley to create the leaf motifs and emblems which now adorn the panelling. Beaune's carpenter/sculptor Pierre Izembart was put in charge of the chapel's new closure. Shifted to the Hall of the Poor (in order for the Hotel-Dieu's funeral processions to be more discreet), it was no longer made of wrought iron but of oak, and found inspiration in the 15th century woodwork designs that are still in place. Maurice Ouradou's drawings provide extremely precise details of the carpentry, joinery, metalwork, sculpture and painting elements, including furniture - such as the beds' sinking clams and florets. This was not done to please tourists, but to restore the original decor of an institution that has been dedicated to the same mission since its foundation: providing care to patients. On 9 December 1878, patients returned to the entirely renovated Grand Hall of the Poor which now had heating...

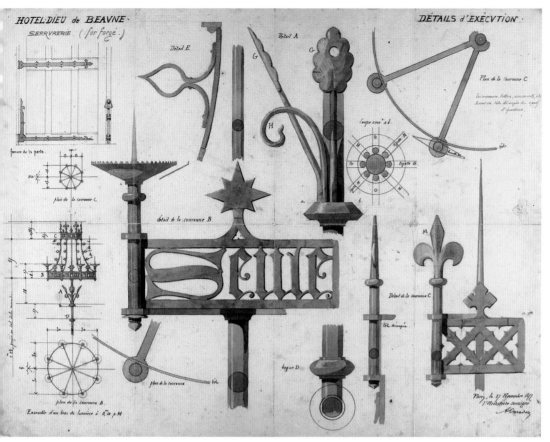

Maurice Ouradou
Hotel-Dieu in Beaune, metalwork
1877, watercolour drawing
The wall sconces made of cut sheet metal are currently visible in the chapel.

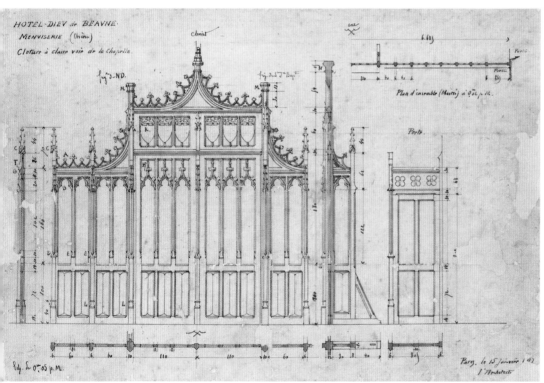

Maurice Ouradou
Hotel-Dieu in Beaune, carpentry
1875, watercolour drawing
Slatted fence of the chapel, reproduced according to the 1501 inventory. This model was made of oak.

EVERY THIRD SUNDAY OF NOVEMBER, AN INTERNATIONAL GATHERING

An auction for a righteous cause

BY RAFAEL PIC
Journalist

Right from the start, and in the spirit of their founder, chancellor Rolin, the Hospices have been able to count on the generosity of many benefactors. This has enabled the Hospices to develop a sizeable private estate, including both real estate and land. In this region, which is famous for its wine, the legacies of vineyards were decisive: although the first one dates back to 1457 - Guillemette, widow of Humbert Le Verrier left 6 ouvrées, which is a quarter of a hectare - they are still productive. In 2010 again, U.S. importer William D. Friedberg donated 6,000 square metres of Santenay. In 2011, Jean-Luc Bissey, a winemaker from the Côte de Nuits, bequeathed 4,000 square metres of Échezeaux, whose production will be sold for the first time at auction on 18 November 2012.

The Hospices' domain currently includes around 60 hectares, mainly around Beaune but also further: in the Côte de Nuits area with the vintage wines of Échezeaux, Mazy-Chambertin and Clos-de-la-Roche, offered respectively by Jean Collignon in 1976, the Cyrot-Chaudron couple and the Kriter couple in 1991, or in the Mâcon area (4 hectares of Pouilly-Fuissé bequeathed in 1994 by Françoise Poisard). Under the authority of a chief of cultures who also fulfils winemaker duties, the Hospices' twenty-two winemaking employees tend to this land which is planted mainly with Pinot Noir (for red wine) and Chardonnay (for white wine), and they follow the principles of integrated viticulture, keeping yields low (less than 35 hectolitres per hectare), which is synonymous with quality.

Once the harvest is complete, fermentation takes place in a new fermentation cellar built in 1994, near the hospital. The original thing about the Hospices' production is the way it sells its wine. After having operated under a bidding system, and having tried conducting auctions, with little success, the Hospices made a decisive decision in the middle of the 19th century, at the urging of Joseph Pétasse, the institution's bursar. Striding across Europe, he managed to sell the entire stock. Upon his return in 1851, he uttered these prophetic words: "Gentlemen, you may resume the public auction process this year; we no longer have to worry, we now have our client base, our wines are known and now it is the wine enthusiasts who will come to us." The success has since been undeniable, and the annual rendezvous on the 3rd Sunday of November is now considered one of the biggest charity auctions in the world. On Friday, Saturday and Sunday mornings, wine tastings are held for both wine professionals and enthusiasts. Saturday night features the chapter of the Knights of Tastevin at the Vougeot enclosed field, Sunday offers an evening gala at the Hospices and Monday features the traditional Paulée de Meursault banquet. The auction starts on Sunday at

14:30 and is held within the setting of Beaune's covered market. It is open to wine lovers from around the world and, for each of the 45 cuvées, entire barrels (228 litres or 288 bottles) are sold off. Traditionally, a barrel - or piece - of wine is sold outside of the catalogue under the sponsorship of a VIP (Otto de Habsbourg, Mstislav Rostropovitch, Charlotte Rampling, Catherine Deneuve, Fabrice Luchini...), for the benefit of a charity organisation.

Beyond their charitable dimension, the Hospices' auctions, conducted since 2005 by Christie's, are the Burgundy wine region's primary communication vehicle and they provide an indication of the vintage's quality. In 2010, the 150th edition was preceded by wine tastings in China, devoted to the international aspect of the auction. The largest quantity sold was in 2009 (799 units) and the record amount raised was in 2000 (€5.2 million). Some cuvées reach spectacular prices. In 2010, although the average price of a unit was €6,922, the Clos-de-la-Roche Cyrot-Chaudron climbed to €40,667 and the Dame des Flandres cuvées of Bâtard-Montrachet went for €63,000. The Hospices' administration has reserved the right to cancel its annual auction, as they did in 1956 and 1968 due to the poor harvest: the great annual November meeting can only allow the highest quality to be auctioned off...

Hospices of Beaune wine auction
November 2011 © Christie's
Since 2005, Christie's (here with François de Ricqlès working the hammer) organises the annual auction.

as a pledge of quality,
yields are kept
under 35 hectolitres
per hectare.

at the Hospices' auctions,
the only units available
are 228-litre barrels.

The hospital in the 21st century

The project initiated by chancellor Rolin more than five centuries ago is still based on the same values: welcoming, alleviating and rescuing. Indeed, it is the hospital of Beaune that receives the final proceeds from the visits to the Hotel-Dieu and from the annual wine auction. The institution is comprised of several structures. The most important one is the Philip the Good short-stay hospital, which was inaugurated on 21 April 1971, and was a landmark achievement in terms of the speed of its construction (18 months) and the technique used (a curtain wall system), as testified by president Pompidou's visit of the work site in 1970. The hospital features 200 beds, its medical emergency department treats 20,000 people a year. In addition to this hospital, the institution's other establishments include: the Nicolas Rolin centre, which opened in 1984 for the dependent elderly (120 beds), the Hotel-Dieu and the Charité's retirement homes (170 beds in the city centre), and the Nursing education institute. Since 1993, there is also a satellite medical facility in the city for those who are most in need. Although the Hospices' hospital activities are financed by Social Security, as is the case with all of France's public health facilities, the income derived from their historical and viticultural heritage facilitates the essential investments that need to be made, particularly in terms of medical equipment and hospital buildings.

Useful information

Hospices of Beaune

Musée de l'Hôtel-Dieu
Rue de l'Hôtel-Dieu – place de la Halle
BP 40104
21203 Beaune Cedex
Open every day of the year

Ticket office hours

In high season (mid-March to mid-November): from 9:30 to 18:30. The rest of the year: from 9:00 to 11:30 and from 14:00 to 17:30. The museum remains open 1 hour after the ticket office has closed.

Visiting the museum

Unaccompanied tour with availability of an audio guide (available in ten languages), or guided tours for groups (1 hour). In July and August, guided tours for individuals are possible.
Rates, information and reservations
10:00 to 12:00 and 14:00 to 16:00
except Saturdays, Sundays and public holidays
Tel.: +33 (0) 3 80 24 45 00
Fax: +33 (0) 3 80 24 45 99
Email: hospices.beaune@ch-beaune.fr
Website: www.hospices-de-beaune.com

The cultural shop

It features a selection of books, gifts and wines harvested on the domains belonging to the Hospices of Beaune.

Books

- *Les Hospices de Beaune en dates et en chiffres (The Hospices of Beaune in dates and figures),* by Bruno François, Jean-Paul Gisserot Publishing, 2012.

- *L'Hôtel-Dieu de Beaune (The Hotel-Dieu in Beaune),* collective work, Somogy art publications, 2005.

- *Guigone de Salins 1403-1470,* by Marie-Thérèse Berthier and John-Thomas Sweeney, Armançon Publishing, 2008.

- *Le chancelier Rolin (Chancellor Rolin) 1376-1462,* by Marie-Thérèse Berthier and John-Thomas Sweeney, Armançon Publishing, 2005.

This work is a publication of **BEAUX ARTS/TTM ÉDITIONS** • 3 carrefour de Weiden, 92130 Issy-les-Moulineaux, France, Tel.: +33 (0)1 41 08 38 00, Fax: +33 (0)1 41 08 38 49, www.beauxartsmagazine.com, RCS Paris B 435 355 896 • **PRESIDENT** Thierry Taittinger • **DIRECTING-EDITOR** Claude Pommereau • **DIRECTOR OF PARTNERSHIPS** Marion de Flers • **ART DIRECTOR** Bernard Borel • **EDITOR IN CHIEF** Rafael Pic • **GRAPHIC DESIGN** Xavier Henry • **ICONOGRAPHER** Alexandra Buffet • **PRODUCT MANAGER** • Charlotte Ullmann • **COPY EDITOR** Julie Houis • **DISTRIBUTION MANAGER** Florence Hanappe • **THE FOLLOWING INDIVIDUALS CONTRIBUTED TO THIS PUBLICATION:** Catherine Baradel-Vallet, Claudine Hugonnet-Berger, Rafael Pic, Claude Pommereau and Thomas Schlesser • **WE WISH TO THANK THE FOLLOWING INDIVIDUALS FOR THEIR VALUABLE ASSISTANCE** Bruno François, Martine Jacquet • **ISBN** 9782-84278-956-5 • **COPYRIGHT** August 2012 • **PHOTOENGRAVING** Litho Art New, Turin • **PRINTED IN FRANCE** • **BOOK STORE DISTRIBUTION: CLIENTS UD,** Flammarion Diffusion commandesclients@union-distribution.fr, Tel. +33 (0)1 41 80 20 20, **OTHER LIBRAIRIES,** Anaïs Guillotte, Tel. : 01 41 08 38 04 • **MAIL ORDER SALES DIP** - Beaux Arts magazine, 18/24, quai de la Marne, 75164 Paris Cedex 19, France, Tel.: +33 (0)1 44 84 80 38 • **CREDITS** © Beaux Arts éditions/TTM Éditions, 2012 • **FOR ALL IMAGES** © Tom Galorbe pg. 2, pg. 4-5, pg. 10, pg. 11, pg. 12, pg. 14, pg. 15, pg. 16, pg. 17 (top left, top right, bottom right), pg. 18, pg. 19 (middle left, middle right, bottom), pg. 20, pg. 21, pg. 22, pg.23, pg. 24, pg. 25, pg. 26 (top right), pg. 27, pg. 36, pg. 38 (top), pg. 39 (top right, bottom), pg. 41 (bottom), back cover • © Didier Piquer - de.me. ter. Editor pg. 17 (bottom left), pg. 19 (haut), pg. 26 (bottom right), pg. 34-35 (top), pg. 34 (bottom), pg. 35 (bottom right), pg. 37 • © Hotel-Dieu in Beaune pg. 7, pg. 8, pg. 13, pg. 29, pg. 30-31, pg. 32-33, pg. 35 (bottom left), pg. 38 (bottom), pg. 39 (top left, middle), pg. 41 (top), pg. 42, pg. 43 • © Rafael Pic pg. 26 (top left) • © Christie's pg. 40 • © Hotel-Dieu in Beaune/ Bruno François p. 41 (top), p. 42.

PEFC
PEFC/10-31-1142